Dancing in The Depths Of my Soul

A BOOK OF POEMS BY ANDY PIVARNIK

© Andy Pivarnik
ajpivarnikova@yahoo.com
724-698-6030

In memory of:
Francine L Cray
and
Marla Pivarnik

CONTENTS:

The Beginning

- White
- To be held
- Written in Stone
- The Stain
- Look up
- Alone
- Blue Wind
- Empty Dreams
- Restoration
- You never left
- In a dream
- One look
- Seeds
- Passion
- Between the days
- Take them back
- The Lie
- cover
- a pinch of salt
- Lunch

Short Stuff'

- Futile
- Truth vs Darkness
- Now
- My all

- Run with it
- Can you see?
- Threshold

No Compromise.........No Regrets

- You
- The Walk
- Tell me I'm wrong
- WTF
- Both
- Buried alive
- Chalk lines in the sky
- This
- Liquid visions
- Next time
- Quiet Fear
- Quiet Fear; Epilogue
- Final Chapter

Thank "YOU";
for the connection, the love, the passion...the dreams...and the timeless inspiration

The Beginning

White

I hate the snow, but the white?
Oh the white!
It covers the dirt, the sin
Fresh, clean, purity
Gods' reminder of forgiveness

But the blank white sheet of paper
It waits
It waits to be covered with words
Words that tell stories of valiant heroes
And desperate sinners

Words that soothe the soul and wash your heart with tears,
Unveil your fears and drop snowflakes of joy
That touches your tongue with healing

White brightens the night with a reflection of truth
The truth of the purest white
That can never be seen by your eyes
But only your heart
Love

To be held

Someone tell me if there is a more
beautiful song than a newborn baby's cry
crying can be rewarding
their cry can bring food right to their crib
but if they are lucky...very lucky
they will be held and loved

but isn't that what we all really want?
from out of the womb
to our last breath
if only
we can be held and loved

Written In Stone

Fate…Destiny...Chance…
It's in the stars
There are many ways of
Describing our life paths
How, at times, we decide
To give ourselves to someone or something
Or close our eyes to what is before us
And let dreams pass us by.

Some would say that
Our life is already set…
We just walk through,
predetermined.
But what of free will,
our ability to choose?
How do we determine
our choices?

Or is that our lives are, written in stone?
I believe that if we truly open our
hearts and look inside,
we can see our paths..
for our future is not
written in stone
but on the heart of man
by the finger of God.

The Stain

As I held her, she wept
Her tears fell and rested on my shoulder
the tears of fear transformed to tears of joy
love can do that

as we separated I wiped the tears from her cheek,
she looked up with a warm thank you in her eyes

later as I changed I noticed a stain on my shirt
where her tears found their home
I thought I'll soak it and wash it out,
then I hesitated for a moment
and thought of how quickly we want to remove the
stains from our lives.

Stains remind us of our mistakes, broken trust, the pain
of misguided love,
rejection and the wrongs that we have done to others in
our selfish ways.

There is a need, we feel, to remove the stains from the
fabric of our hearts
as if they were never there,
but they are!

God tells us he will wipe away every tear,
but what of the stains?

Maybe they should stay
to remind us of our life journey.
our failures and joys, in that they
define us, mold us and build us.

That our choices mean something;

to us, the people in our lives and in God's love for us and that every stain marks a change in the direction of our heart.

Look up

Today when you walk out your door…look up!
See that blue sky?
I see the same!
Feel that sun
Touch your face?
I feel the same!
And if you feel so inclined
Look to that cloud passing by
And say "Hi"
I'll hear you

Alone

There are times in our lives when the word
"alone "is inadequate in describing the deepness
of the pain and the darkness that we dwell in

not the darkness of evil, but darkness
of being lost;
someone misdirected you and
words that at one time lifted you up,
caused your heart to leap
and brought joy and the promise of
love and happiness
those words now echo in your mind,
hollow and without meaning, torturing

trust and truth have been
dismantled

dreams turn into nightmares,
at times it feels as though you have to
think in order to breath

how can something so perfect,
so connected, so magical
... just end
alone

Blue Wind

I sense your sweet smell, on the breath of the morning breeze
I seek your name in the stillness of the night
I listen for your voice in the silence of the moonlight
But there is no sound
Only a blue wind that surrounds me
Chilling doubt
But I believe

I feel your tenderness in the fragile delicacy a single leaf
I see your smile in the sun shining brightly
And in the eyes of a birthday child
But you are not
My arms are empty
You've chosen to end at only the start
A feeling that warmed my heart like a blanket of love
Complete..soft…and real, is gone

For in the loneliness of the night
The emptiness of my heart fills the sky
Yet I have hope
That in a new day, when the sun rises
And you feel your heart leaning towards me
Ride that blue wind to my waiting arms

Distance

Can you feel me in your dreams?
Held deep within my arms
Endless nights cut short
By a choice that's not my own

Is there safety in the number
Of days that pass without you?

Time cannot weaken the love
I have tried to bury
It lives on in the shadow of your leaving

Clouds of sorrow darken my footsteps
With hope barely shining thru
And as the sun rises in the morning
So do my memories of you

Empty Dreams

At the end of each day
In the quiet of the moon
I listen to what my heart has to say
It echoes in an empty room
For my heart has left
Its beat is but a memory

The other night, while I was sleeping
I heard your voice softly call my name
I turned to see you there, then
With a smile you asked me to kiss you
And at the touch of your lips
I awaken to emptiness beside me

With the thought of you, tears fill my eyes
Like water fills a vase
The sweet smell of a summer rain
Brings memories of holding you close
With your sent filling my senses

But as the summer gives way to autumn
And autumn to winter
The seasons of my life
Without you fall cold

Restoration

Shadows beside me
a place where she once walked
I've been forgotten, cast aside
I was cherished and adored
now my emotions are tattered,
ignored and mocked.

Love has been victimized,
trust suffered a silent death
and what of hope?
words that screamed of passion
that created a future of shared dreams
now weigh heavily on my mind
sinking those dreams into
the depths of despair.

Desperation has led me to a
Sorrowful path, thick with lies
and empty promises
now as my last drop of hope is lost
in a sea of tears
I am failing
growing weaker every day
until I stop...

As I lay there; my body,
sprit and soul sink deep into the earth
covered ..protected
slowly I am....reborn anew
love has saved me....restored me
until I can stand again
and walk.

You never left

I haven't heard your voice
or touched your face
in far too long.
the days creep,
slowly reminding me
that you're not with me
you're not by my side
or in my arms.

And I haven't tasted your sweet lips
to quench my thirst,
but then as the sun sleeps
and my tired eyes shut
you appear…

True love visits me in my dreams
my soul smiles
its mate is back
your touch is real
and the face that lit up
my world the first time we met
draws close.

As your caring eyes
swallow me up in a pool
of passion,
my mind and heart agree
to let you return
with joy and love
hand in hand...
that is until the daylight
my eyes open and you're gone...

So I wait for you
when the night falls once again
and you return
it is now that I see that
you never left
that place in my heart
where no other can dwell
is where you will always be.

The movement of your lips
the softness of your touch,
the touch that runs through me
a direct current to my heart.
they wait till the dreams awake them..
and you,
you visit me again.

In a dream

In a dream
Seconds – time – a life

A man near death can live a long life,
See his son he loves become a man
And his grandchildren play

A lame child runs a race with the wind
And a lonely woman holds the baby
Of her love with a warm embrace

A motherless child is covered by the
Parents she always dreamed she knew

A world filled with greed, anger and
Immorality in the name of freedom;
Will have peace, love and joy
In the eyes of the Dream -maker

One look

As if taken from my mind's eye, there she was
Perfection in its closet form…untouchable
Her shape has a smoothness I can taste
Flowing in a direction, so sensuous my hands tremble
Eyes with the awe of a newborn baby,
Yet able to see the secrets of my emotions
With a presence that pleases the eye, the heart and soul
She touches with a warmth one cannot learn

Her hair, scattered with sunshine, falls gently
On her shoulders, like a shower of silken rain
She smiles with the freshness of a summer night,
Speaking passicn without saying a single word
So what can I do with this vision of love?
I wonder and wait to see if her hand touches mine.

Seeds

As we are walking through the pastures of our lives
We are witness to the harvest of time
How were we to know the product of our seeds?
The violence in our streets and the fear in our hearts
Are children born in prejudice, can we choose right from wrong
Tell me who planted the product of our seeds?

Families disenchanted fall apart too soon
Giving way to pressures that bring a strong man down
The colors of our lives are blanketed with gray
What is evil, what is good
Tell me who's to say
The answer is the evidence of our seeds

Some are birthed from seeds of love some are birthed in hate
Are we defined by who we are or by how much we make
Do we fill the void in a homeless child?
Or rape the land for progress sake?
What we see and dream is the product of our seeds

At what price do we find ourselves?
Greed as means of reaching higher goals
At the cost of morals we show our children how to live for oneself
In the land of youth grow the product of our seeds

We need a restoration of our souls, a healing of the heart
A soothing touch from the winds of peace

Today's the birth of tomorrow's dreams, will the future harvest weeds?
Let's not forget to look within
For we are the sowers of the seeds

Passion

In the depths of passion
There is a pain to be found

With language that fills a fool's
Ears with love's hope and promise

Only to be empty words
That falls lifeless to the ground

Still your presence follows me
Like a shadow; silent and dark
Covering my past
Questioning my future

Connected to the deepest part of me
Yet! Without substance and cold as moonlight

Love without end, its beginning unknown
Lives on in the desert of my heartbreak

Alone, unseen and unwanted by the one
That planted the seed of passion,
You

Between the days

Time starts before my waking day
Piling up my losses in endless shades of gray
Pain covers my heart
With a blanket of doubt
So dark, that I can't find my way out
And the doors of my escape
Are sealed with lies

Between the days
I find my peace, my freedom
And joy is by my side
A tear…a smile …together
My heart is wide open
Can I stay?
Please, I don't want to leave!!
But No, another day arrives

Take them back

I'd like to take the words I said to you
And put them back inside

Take away the hurt I put you through
And replace it with a smile

There are things I'd do so differently
And things I wouldn't do

But, I sit and watch the colors of my life
Turning pale and gray

People walking by me on the streets
In shallow depths of sound

Time, they say, will heal a broken heart
But what does a heart know of time

The Lie

He's walking with a lie in his hand
In the silence of the night
"Come on in, it feels real fine"
How can this be wrong?
But the fact of your decision is
It seldom turns out right

Yes we have an agreement,
A partnership is made
If I'm to do all of this,
Then what is it you do?

Love full of empty promises
Then the fear of idol threats
"Deception" leaves you wondering
Whose reality this is

Cover

when the echo of unkept promises
are deafening
and the shadows of yesterdays
pain and failures
are so heavy
that each step seems impossible to make,
throw off the weight
and cover yourself with hope...
of which doubt has no grip

A pinch of salt

The nature of life is
a recipe that is ever changing

If we do not suffer
and experience pain...
how then can we appreciate
joy and happiness

without rejection....
the open arms of acceptance
would not be recognized

it's when we are lost in the cold darkness
of heartbreak...
that the light and warmth of love
can show us our path and
point us in the direction of truth

to hold true love..
is to hold everything
that you ever wanted or dreamed of

but to truly live...
one must put to death
fear and doubt
and cast the light of hope
upon the next step
towards tomorrow

LUNCH

A softly lit diner
with an atmosphere that smells of home
or at least a friendly rest stop
on this unknown journey

good coffee and
real utensils that reflect
the years of a welcoming voice
and kind hands

in a small booth
is a woman with a look that only comes from the winds
of time,
that push us forward...
sits alone
slow deliberate movements
as she eats quietly
glancing up now and then
and smiling
at the memory that sat across from her
more times than not

a table of four,
midway through this timeless eatery,
is filled with endless movement
and laughter
sits a young couple
with a newborn and his older sister....
who's antics brighten the
babes eyes with undeniable joy
mom and dad ...smile

at a corner table..

sitting with an empty chair across from him
is a man who's gaze leads somewhere else
his plate appears untouched and cold

set in the front, near the entrance,
adolescent conversation
with neither listening
as both are speaking words
that never catch up to their thoughts

what appears to be a table set aside
from the rest of the world...
a middle aged couple sit
unaware of the movement around them
taking each other in
through the eyes of open hearts
subtle smiles
one hand barely touching the other
with wanting finger tips...
in soundless conversation...
only the parting of lips
and the focus of the one receiving the message
give way to this exchange of passion

strangers sharing a common space
for uncommon reasons
consuming a small piece of each other's lives
with sweeping looks and passing thoughts

so open the door
to this culinary gathering
have a seat....
meet me for lunch

Short Stuff

Futile
….the efforts of man are futile in the vastness of time, but the heart of man holds the truth of his existence

Truth vs Darkness
…timeless is the light of truth in the darkness of hate and despair.

Now
So this is NOW!
Not later or before
But NOW!
I see things that I have never seen before
The last thought is the best thought that leads to movement
Prior to that it was just an idea
Ideas without movement equals frustration
A slippery thought that you just can't get a hold of

My all
When I gave all my love
I never feared loss
only that
I didn't give enough

Run with it
Love like there is no tomorrow
Dream like the world will never end

Can you see?

The eye of the soul
cannot see clearly
through a mind of logic..
only through a transparent heart
can it see true love

Threshold

……beyond the door of the unknown lies the answer
that man refuses to embrace

No Compromise......No Regrets

You

An unexpected meeting with unbelievable results
Suddenly everything around me vanished
All that I could see or hear was you

Something inside me jumped
My heart stopped and watched
What was this connection?

Lightning struck!
And there was dancing in the depths of my soul

You were there in front of me
My arms aching to hold but unable to move

Amazed of what was happening
I attempted to put it into words;
Fate? God? My Soul mate?
Or was this the inevitable, and the time was now - for "us"?

At times it's as if I have known you all along,
My friend.....the common thread in my life, my first love

All that matters is now with you.
I watch you talk and every movement of your face,
From the twitch of your nose to the softness of your lips,
Parting just enough to release your words
And the voice that has become music to my ears

To hold you is to hold two hearts beating as one
A sense of, "Yes!" that I have never felt before

A day without you

Is like a day without the sun
Dark and cold

Stay for now, in this man's life, maybe you'll stay forever

The Walk

I have walked in the shadows of my secrets,
I have walked in the light of truth
 At times enjoyed acceptance,
only to feel the chill of rejection.....
undiscussed pain

Time wasted with tears of love lost,
answers await me,
but the questions keep them afar
Then for some unknown, unseen
and unexpected reason
YOU

a part of me that I never met
but always knew was
there..in front of me
I hear my heart....my soul
calling for yours
beating in rhythm with your sweet breath
let us walk
and chase our dream together

Tell me I'm wrong!

At the start
the connection was magical, like her
electric…energy one could feel
like no other time in my life,
and I've been around,
but never around anything like this

we moved quickly, as if controlled by a stronger force
than either one of us has ever encountered

each day was better than the last
conversations lasted for hours
but felt like only minutes had passed
when we were together, my heart would flutter,
dancing….my hands would sweat, aching to hold her
she filled my eyes with joy

my soul was saying…this is it,
and her soul agreed

finally I could tell my heart…open up fully and freely,
and allow this romance to come alive,
one that has waited for her,
to treat her as she has always dreamed
with the deepest love that has no end

then suddenly, the brakes of caution were applied..
agreeing to slow it down, I tried to control this energy
to stretch out the learning curve on this relationship,

get to know each other like normal people do.
But the problem is...neither of us are normal
and for sure this connection...this energy.

this accident of fate, was far from normal
could it exist at a slower pace?
would it be able to breathe or would it
suffocate...unable to run free?

at first....it was fine...slower but just as satisfying
the dreams of "us" still lived..
but then...the conversations became quicker...shorter
they lessened
then they stopped!!
attempts to talk had no reply
questions had no answers

how can this happen?

this magic ..this gift from God
this one in a million meeting of the souls
was becoming...normal?
an empty feeling entered the deepest part of me

without her voice each day, just for a moment..."Hi"
"goodnight my love"..."I miss you"
assuring me that she was mine
and her desire for me...for "us"
was still strong as from the start,
hope started to fade...dreams blurred

Was our love, my truelove,
walking away?
tell me I'm wrong

WTF

The uneasiness in the deepest part of me
worry
It eats through my mind,
looking to devour hope!
something...someone has cut the connection
Why?

My soul looks but can't find its match
its other half,
is it gone for good?
or just in hiding?

hiding from the truth that true love will reveal,
its weakness
its fears
the issues that no one has seen and few have heard,
untold but to a few
marks in the path of this life
that constantly remind of failure and pain.

Come close.
Let "the kiss" open your eyes again
to the possibilities
get caught in "the embrace" that will melt
the broken dreams of the past that darken your vision.

Stay close.
Hold on.
Hearts and souls as one,
embrace each other and each day,
the days that lead to forever

Both

It's a fact; the same one who brought
immeasurable joy
has left me in stinging darkness

from having a future for "us"; with the promise
of dreams yet to be dreamt;
to questions with no answers,
empty pages...

the heart, slain by the hand that once held it close;
silent, yet alive
my skin aches, affected by
the pain that radiates from my torn soul
throughout my very being

but,
then...
silence
awaiting for the return of
love....
my resurrection

Buried alive

I'm so weary
It's been a long day
I need to rest....but,

what if she's there..
when I close my eyes..
what if I hear her voice...
echoing from the shallow grave
that she buried our love..."us"

"us"..
it was a word that when she spoke it..
a light of hope and promise
filled my heart and soul..
she was the focus of my passion..
the target of my affection..
the object of my desire

the night would always end
with her tender voice..
touching off dreams..
that continued the conversation

I would awake with a smile
and a sense of "yes"!
when I lifted myself from the bed
and my feet touched the floor...
the earth moved!

Chalk lines in the sky

chalk lines in the sky..
brush lines from the winds hand..
 I see your face

In the breeze
the whisper of your voice
softens my day
a sweet song in my heart

I couldn't hold you close enough...
long enough

my love for you is squeezing my soul
painfully strong
bleeding warmly over my being...
covering me

I reach for the sky to touch you,
as a tree reaches for freedom
my roots are so deep
that they touch the other side of reality

This

Sometimes I wonder
if the magical connection
with this woman that dwells
in the deepest cavern of my soul
and my love for her was real

Maybe my mind, my heart and my spirit,
unbeknownst to me,
one day decided they would get together..
and create something so beautiful,
so amazing,
that it would touch me in a way I've never been touched
before.

And in doing so,
created a hunger and a creative flow
that has changed my direction..
my vision...
my life.

That being said,
what do I do with this love,
this passion and desire for a woman that may have never
been?

I will allow it to live...
to grow stronger with every beat!

It will be challenged for sure
but it will challenge the doubt and fear
of those whose dreams
have been turned into nightmares
by others with darken hearts.

But even the darkest of hearts
cast a shadow because of the light of truth.

a shadow that is ever changing...
until the light is right overhead..
then the shadow is consumed
by the source of its own existence..

liquid visions

My thoughts are covered with
the heaviness of memories
that push through my mind
as if a hat that's made of dark matter
sits on my head

squeezing liquid visions of loves blurred remains
out from behind the walls
of my safe haven

my eyes are shut
but I still see

dancing lights....
crack through the darkness
reveling the visions
in a staccato movement

rain surrounds me
like glass bars
confining me..
yet...reflecting where I am
and where I have been

with patient willingness.....
one strategic step forward at a time
on an uncharted path,
I walk until the walls are shattered
so I can reach the dreams
that await me

Next Time

Forgive me but, I have a problem!
It's you!

It's not what you think,
you're not a problem,
you're the solution
to the puzzle of my scattered dreams

you are the fuel that moves me
the problem is....
I can't get enough of you!

knowing your fingers
touched a key pad
to send me a message
only increases my want
hearing your voice..
will calm my rapidly beating heart,
but only for a moment .

then my desire craves more
my eyes only focus is you
my arms ache for your body
but you're not near!

my ears hear silence
my eyes see only
the picture of you that hangs on the walls of my soul,
that is..
until the next time, my love, until the next time

Quiet Fear

There is a place in your heart,
if you're not careful,
where fear will hide.
It stays lifeless and quiet
until...it smells "true love",
fear hates true love,
the love that souls desire;

A magical connection
of unknown source
made before time itself
a sense of oneness
beyond oneness
unexplainable but real,
as if the two were
birthed from the same spiritual womb

Then when the once separate souls see that they
are becoming "us" and the exchange between them
becomes one voice!
Fear quietly awakens.

It starts with a whisper
"you're moving too fast, too much too soon"'
as if love has a certain pace
one must adhere to, but
one of the souls listens
and the flame is lessened.

Now fear has the one thinking with their head
and not follow the heart,
so as fear then subtly throws doubt
on the table of unknown conversation.

Now the words are escaping from
the doors of the past...pain....mistrust,
backed up by a voice that says,
"I'm not ready"...."I can't do this"
The two souls from one womb
Connection is pulled…stretched to the point
of breaking...
then one soul lets go....
turns and walks back to the place

behind its walls...safe as before,
before "true love" came and
knocked the walls down.
Now the walls are back,
custom built by fear itself.

So between the two separated souls
lies "true love"
barely breathing...fading...dying
until its torn heart is barely beating....then quiet...
Fear is dancing; he's defeated "true love"
Then, suddenly, fear feels a sharp pain in his ears ..the sound of
a heartbeat...true and strong
....."true love" lives

Quiet Fear; Epilogue

Fears closest friend, Doubt, was feeling rather good about himself,
he and Fear may not have killed true love,
but they did separate the two souls from one womb.
Doubt turned and with a smirk, questioned Hope,
who was seated and gently holding the wounded true love;
"so what now of the connection between true love...truth and passion?"
Hope slowly looked up and with a glimmer of a smile said;
"the heart wants what the heart wants"!

Final Chapter

The sun warms my face
and a cool breeze
washes over me,
a cleansing breath from above
but my soul is alone
my heart beats slowly
with only the echo
of her voice keeping it
from stopping.

Oh foolish passion what have you done?
you panicked and went rushing in
instead of patiently waiting.
when she let go of you and turned,
you, in fear, screamed out
with no clear reply
you screamed even louder
drowning out her words.

Confused you reached out
to take back your dream
only to push it away
maybe if you would have just listened,
backed off and given her the space and time
she asked for
we would not be sitting here alone,
without her by our side or
perhaps it was fear...or
just the simple fact that
"the want" had vanished!

For whatever the reason
wherever you are, my dear soul mate;

forgive my misled passion
that was driven by fear
and unbound desire.
you will be in my heart forever
in a place untouched by another.

la parola finale dell'amore

....out of the depths of pain......beauty can emerge

Made in the USA
Columbia, SC
25 February 2018